# This book belongs to...

Name: ______________________



Address: ____________________________________

City: _________ State: _____ Zip Code: _________

Phone: ___________ Email: ____________________

www.ingramcontent.com/pod-product-compliance
Lightning Source LLC
Chambersburg PA
CBHW051325220526
45468CB00004B/1496